NEW VANGUARD • 175

US SUBMARINES 1900–35

JIM CHRISTLEY   ILLUSTRATED BY PETER BULL

First published in Great Britain in 2011 by Osprey Publishing,
Midland House, West Way, Botley, Oxford, OX2 0PH, UK
44-02 23rd St, Suite 219, Long Island City, NY 11101, USA

E-mail: info@ospreypublishing.com

A CIP catalogue record for this book is available from the British Library

ISBN: 978 1 84908 185 6
E-book ISBN: 978 1 84908 186 3

Page layout by Melissa Orrom Swan, Oxford
Index by Mike Parkin
Typeset in Sabon and Myriad Pro
Originated by PDQ Digital Media Solutions, Suffolk, UK
Printed in China through Worldprint Ltd

11 12 13 14 15   10 9 8 7 6 5 4 3 2 1

Osprey Publishing is supporting the Woodland Trust, the UK's leading
woodland conservation charity by funding the dedication of trees.

www.ospreypublishing.com

CONTENTS

US SUBMARINES 1900–35

INTRODUCTION

This book is an introduction to the early years of the US Naval Submarine Force, covering mainly the period 1900 to 1935. Even though there is little mention of other countries, inventors and navies here it should be understood that the US did not invent and develop a submarine force in a vacuum and that there were not only earlier, but also parallel, programs all over the world.

The submarine as a naval weapon faced a problem early on in its development, which was that of propulsion. Early attempts at submarines used human power, compressed air, steam and other propulsion methods, with some limited success. The inventive insight of John Phillip Holland led to the combination of an internal combustion engine to provide surface power; an electric motor with power supplied by a storage battery to supply propulsion energy when submerged; and the use of the motor as a generator to charge the battery when the engine could be run on the surface.

This combination of elements, properly arranged, made a workable, fully submerging vessel that, when equipped with a torpedo tube launching an automobile torpedo, was an invisible threat to any unsuspecting capital ship. Holland's submarine was purchased by the US Navy in 1900. By 1930, a mere 30 years later, the concept of submarine warfare had been tested in war and had progressed so far that submarines could range over all the world's oceans and their role was written into the battle plans of all the world's navies.

THE GENESIS OF THE US NAVAL SUBMARINE FORCE

The American Civil War was under way by May 1861, when the Philadelphia police, acting on nervous reports of strange goings-on at the waterfront, arrested the French diver and inventor Brutus de Villeroi, and some of his workmen. They also impounded a curious device. It was an iron tube some 33ft long and about 5ft in diameter. De Villeroi had developed, based on his experiments in France, a submarine which he had hoped to use as a salvage platform. Without doubt the police, not being sure of the patriotic intent of the inventor, had no clear understanding of what this submarine object was, but they knew it needed to be put under the control of the United States Navy. Captain Samuel F. DuPont, commandant of the Philadelphia Navy Yard, was informed about the device. He appointed three officers to examine it, interview the inventor and report their findings to him and the Navy Department.

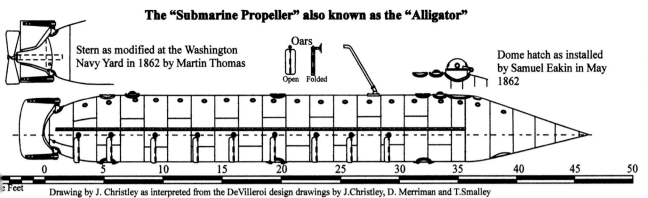

The "Submarine Propeller" also known as the "Alligator"

Stern as modified at the Washington Navy Yard in 1862 by Martin Thomas

Oars
Open   Folded

Dome hatch as installed by Samuel Eakin in May 1862

0   5   10   15   20   25   30   35   40   45   50

Feet

Drawing by J. Christley as interpreted from the DeVilleroi design drawings by J.Christley, D. Merriman and T.Smalley

The small submarine was duly inspected. The result of this inspection was that the Navy contracted a slightly larger version as a possible weapon with which to attack the ironclad CSS *Virginia*, then being built by the Confederacy in the recently captured Gosport navy yard near Norfolk, Virginia. The building of the submarine was fraught with trouble and controversy. However, on May 1, 1862, the "Submarine Propeller," as it was called, was launched by a crane which lowered the boat into the Delaware River. Samuel Eakin was appointed to superintend the boat and finish the details. Finally, it was ready; William Hirst, a Philadelphia lawyer and go-between for de Villeroi, got instructions from Commodore Joseph Smith, Chief of the Bureau of Yards and Docks, to formally turn the boat over to the Commandant of the Philadelphia Navy Yard, a task he completed on June 13, 1862, the true birthdate of the US Naval Submarine Force.

This submarine, painted green on the outside and with its bulbous dome and paddles, resembled an alligator and was so nicknamed. The sobriquet stuck and the boat was referred to in official correspondence as the USS *Alligator*. The boat was deployed to the James River during the latter part of the American Civil War's "Seven Days Campaign" in 1862, but could not

The little submarine known as the *Alligator* was built by the Union Navy in late 1861 and accepted for service in June, 1862. It was deployed in the James River at the end of the US Civil War's Seven Days Campaign. It was lost off the North Carolina coast in April 1863 while being towed south to be used to attack Charleston, South Carolina. No crewmen were aboard. (Author's collection)

The USS *Holland* in drydock after being commissioned. The type seen here is very much like the Skipjack-Class fast-attack nuclear submarine of the 1960s. The man standing just forward of the flagstaff provides a sense of scale. (Navy History Center)

be used due to the shallowness of the river. It was sent to the Washington Navy Yard for testing and, finally, was put under tow early in 1863 and taken down the Atlantic coast with the aim of aiding the Union Navy's effort to force entry into Charleston harbor, South Carolina. The little submarine was lost in a storm off Cape Hatteras in April, 1863. Early the following year, the Confederate Navy's *H. L. Hunley* became the first submarine to sink an enemy ship in combat.

The US Navy bought another submarine, similar in nature to the *Alligator*, in 1864. It was called the *Intelligent Whale* and served as a test platform for some years, then was forgotten. This submarine, however, still exists – it is on display at the National Guard Museum of New Jersey, and is the oldest existing naval submarine in the world.

THE NAVY'S FIRST MODERN SUBMARINES

The Navy accepted and commissioned the USS *Holland* in October of 1900. It was the first of the unbroken line of commissioned submarines in the US Navy. John Holland had already built a follow-on design, the *Fulton*, which he showed to naval officials. The Navy wanted more boats and put in an order for seven to be built along the lines of the *Fulton*. The first was laid down in New Jersey the following month. By the spring of 1901, all seven were well in hand in two shipyards. On the west coast were the *A-3* and the *A-5* at the Union Iron Works in San Francisco. In Elizabethport, New Jersey, the *A-1*, *A-2*, *A-4*, *A-6* and *A-7* were being built in the Crescent Shipyard.

The construction technique used was different from anything we see today as welding was non-existent. Everything had to be either cast into the desired shape or fabricated from rolled steel, which was then either bolted or riveted together. Frames of rolled T-stock or Z-stock were erected about 18in apart. These frames had pre-drilled, ¾in holes around their periphery. Rolled and hammered, ½in oil-tempered plates, some nearly 70ft long and 8ft wide with tapered ends, were laid against the frames and holes were marked.

A D-Class boat under construction. The building method was not much different from that used in building surface ships. Frames were set up and hull plates riveted in place. The saddle-shaped ballast tanks – patented by the boat's manufacturer, EB – are seen here with the flat floor being the base for the battery cells. It should be remembered that without the welding common to construction today all the parts seen here had to be either cast to shape, rolled and hammered to shape and bolted, or riveted, together. (Ric Hedman, Pigboats.com)

A D-Class engine room looking aft. One can imagine what the environment was like for the enginemen and electricians, with the noise, heat and moving parts. The main propulsion motors are just visible in the lower center. (Ric Hedman, Pigboats.com)

Atop the center of the pressure hull, a large cylindrical casting was inserted. Merely 3ft in diameter, the cylinder was closed at the top by a hatch which was 2ft in diameter. This was the conning tower and, with its small circular windows, served as the only view of the outside world for the commander when the boat was submerged.

The engine was gasoline-fueled and had four cylinders. However, that is where the resemblance to the modern automobile engine ends. The cylinders were about 7in in diameter and had a stroke of nearly a foot. The engine could be turned over by hand, by the electric motor, or air-started. It was started on one cylinder and only as it was turning over would the others be cut in by adjusting the fuel and spark. It had to be tweaked constantly and, as it only ran in one direction, going astern on the engine was out of the question. There was also only a limited speed adjustment. Half speed of about four knots and full speed of about 8½ knots were the choices. The engine would develop 180hp when running properly. The piping system was difficult to maintain as it had flanged fittings bolted up, was pipe thread with only lead paste to form a gasket, and had no swage fittings or compression joints. Lubricating oil was splashed into the bearings in the semi-open crankcase and the oil cups were gravity-fed and had to be reused by filling the oil cups from a can. Working around the engine with all its open moving cams, crankshafts and rods made it a dangerous time to be a machinist.

The battery well in an A-Class submarine. This view shows the open-topped set of battery cells with their plates suspended in the rubber-lined steel cells. The entire arrangement was covered by planks resting on the deck lip seen in the upper portion of the picture. (US Navy SFLM)

Being gasoline-fueled, there were issues with leaks and fumes. The fumes could build up and cause two problems. The first was the obvious fire hazard and any fire would be sudden and disastrous. The second problem was the effect of the fumes on the brain. They tended to accumulate

A USS *Holland* was the first US submarine that successfully combined all the elements that were necessary for a submarine weapon system. Surfaced operation used an internal combustion engine and submerged operation an electric motor for main propulsion. The engine drove a generator (which was the motor) to charge a lead acid battery for submerged operation. An underwater torpedo tube using a Whitehead type torpedo formed the main weapon (the dynamite gun was not repeated in other designs). One element generally overlooked in this design was that it was repeatable, and could thus be offered for sale in quantity.

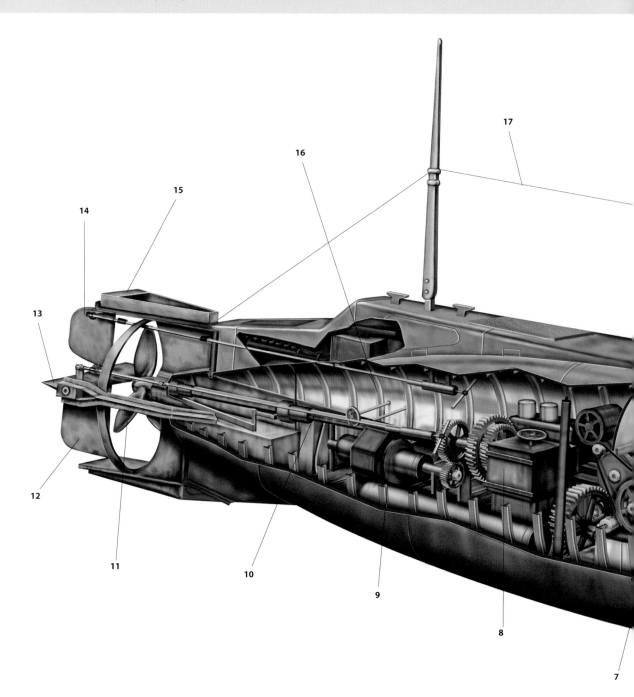

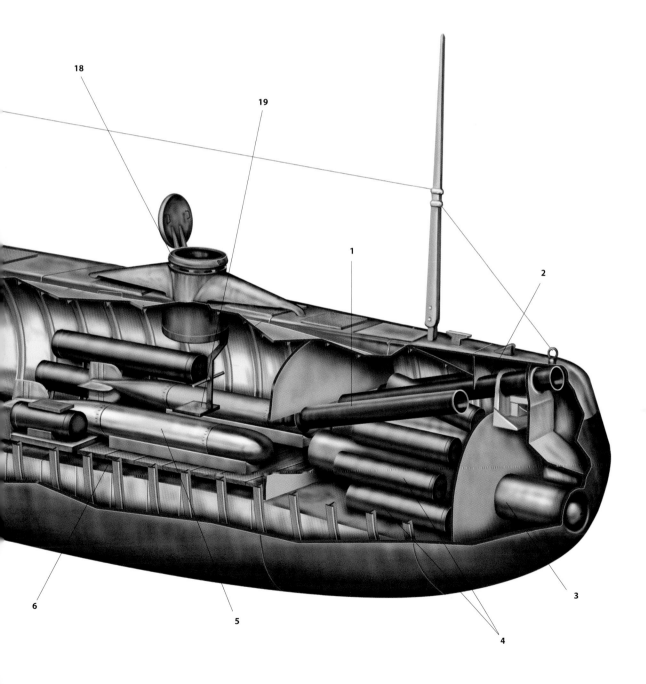

low in the ship and caused displacement of the oxygen and slow asphyxia. The crew affected would have a feeling of euphoria and impaired judgment. Death by suffocation would follow even if no fire broke out.

Aft of the engine on the main shaft was a hand-operated band clutch. Next in line was the 70hp open-yoke DC motor. Powered from the battery, it drove the propeller shaft. It was reversible and had some speed control so it was used for maneuvering near the dock. The shaft also drove, through a set of friction clutches, the air compressor and ballast pump. Full speed submerged was seven knots.

Nestled inside the wings of the main ballast tanks was the battery. It was a lead acid battery, with lead plates and sulfuric acid as the electrolyte. It was the same general type used today. However, there were some significant differences. Today's battery is enclosed in a hard rubber and plastic cell jar that holds the electrolyte and plates. These battery cells were steel boxes lined with a layer of rubber and a layer of lead and wedged in place with waxed maple wedges. The boxes were open-topped and the plates were hung from the top of the cell jar by extenders. The positive plates were connected together with a soldered bus bar of lead-coated copper. The negative plates were hung and connected in a similar manner. The cells were then connected in with bus bars. The cells were wedged in place in the steel box and the box was bounded by the ballast tanks and the fore and aft half-bulkheads. The top of the battery well was covered by shellacked oak planks. The planks, when in place, were covered by a rubber sheet with a shellacked canvas walking cover on top. If any maintenance or monitoring of the battery gravity or temperature had to be done, the planks were temporarily taken up.

The cells could be cut out of the circuit and repaired by replacing acid and plates. The space above the cells was ventilated by air leaking down around the planks which was then drawn off to be exhausted over the side by the battery blowers. When being charged (and to a lesser extent while being discharged at a high rate), the battery generated hydrogen gas. This gas is highly flammable at a four percent concentration in air and explosive at a seven percent concentration. If the battery were improperly charged or improperly ventilated a concentration of hydrogen could build quickly and lead to an explosion.

Another gas generated by the battery was hydrogen sulfide. The rotten-egg smell of this gas permeated everything onboard. Then there was additional issue of chlorine. As stated earlier, the battery was in the center of the boat, covered by a deck of planks, rubber sheet and canvas. Directly above the deck were the conning tower and the main hatch into the boat. The top of the hatch was 5ft above the waterline with the original design and 8ft with the later conning tower design. Any seawater coming down the hatch fell directly onto the battery deck. If any leaked into the cells, the sulfuric acid combined with the sodium chloride in the seawater and liberated a pea-green, heavier-than-air, oxygen-displacing, toxic gas – chlorine. If cells became salted, they were charged and discharged while ventilating the boat to get rid of the chlorine, then new acid was added as necessary.

The troops. A classic view of submariners during World War I. They are atop the fairwater of the *E-2*. The man in the center is sitting on the battery ventilation intake. Behind the men are the two periscopes. Below the right knee of the center man is the radio antenna tap that is connected to the antenna above and to the radio transmitter inside the boat. (Navy History Center)

The battery was connected to a master switchboard. This was a single 3ft-by-4ft slab of 2in-thick marble, supported by steel angle and channel, which was mounted vertically on the starboard side of the boat (or port side on some boats). On this slab were fastened all the switches and rheostats for connecting the battery, dynamo, lights and motors. There were no other switchboards or distribution boxes. That was it. It was all open switches and open wiring. Battery voltage varied from 70 to 160 volts DC. The inside of the boat was either hot and damp or cold and damp. Grounds (earths) were common. It was a dangerous time to be an electrician.

Up front was a single 18in-diameter torpedo tube. The boat could carry one torpedo in the tube and two in the boat on each side of the middle space (where the battery well was). The torpedo man who took care of the torpedoes was a real craftsman. The "fish" was powered by high-pressure air which powered a four-cylinder air motor. It was a straight runner, with only a rudimentary (and not very reliable) depth control. Each fish had to have its gyro set up in the shop and tweaked prior to loading. The "dynamite gun" seen in the *Holland* was omitted in the A-Class design.

The crew consisted of one officer, normally an ensign, and six enlisted men. There would be two chief petty officers; one was the chief electrician and the other the chief machinist. A couple of machinists, another electrician and a torpedo man would round out the crew.

DEVELOPMENT

The Navy was in a quandary about how to buy submarines. Electric Boat Company (EB) had good capital (albeit buttressed by selling patent rights and an interest in the company to Vickers) and was capable of building submarines of good quality in multiples of the same design. Simon Lake (of the Lake Torpedo Boat Company) used a more complex fundamental design which was more difficult to build. He kept changing the design details and thus his boats were not easily reproducible in quantity and by yards other than his own (EB had its designs built by subcontractor yards on both the east and west coasts). It seemed the easy choice would be to simply buy EB submarines. However, that would lead to EB having a controlling monopoly which the Navy wished to avoid.

Early on, the Navy bought EB's standard designs in quantity. Of Lake's boats the Navy bought only three, the *G-1*, *G-2* and *G-3*. In later acquisitions some class purchases were split between the two builders. Thus the L, O and R classes comprised boats designed by both EB and Lake.

The USS *Holland* was the first of what was to be a continuous line of submarines in the US Navy. Its hull form was a teardrop shape which was widely recognized as the form that would give minimum resistance when traveling submerged. Purchased in 1900, the boat was tested extensively. The first multiple-boat purchase was of the A-Class. Four of the boats were built at Elizabethport, New Jersey, at the Crescent Shipyard and two, the *A-3* and the *A-5*, were built at the Union Iron Works in San Francisco, California. As EB owned no building yards at this time the company contracted construction to various yards, then mainly to the Fore River Shipyard in Quincy, Massachusetts. The A-Class was built from EB plans. The plans were John Holland's seventh set, the sixth being those for the *Holland*. The first of the class is normally the one with the lowest class number and the first to be laid down. This was not the case with the A-Class. The *A-1* was the USS *Plunger* and differed slightly from its sisters. The first boat laid down was the *A-2*, the USS *Adder*. Thus the class became known as the "Adders." There was a class prototype built – the *Fulton*. It was tested by EB and when the Navy didn't buy it, EB sold it to Russia to compete with Simon Lake who had already sent his submarine, *Protector*, over and was looking for contracts for more. Lake got a contract and built five boats at Newport News Shipbuilding for the tsar.

USS *Grampus* (right) and USS *Pike* at Mare Island, California. Judging by the pristine condition of the boats and the two officers in dress blue uniform, something important is happening. This may have been taken on commissioning day, May 28, 1903. The bow of the receiving ship USS *Independence* can be seen in the right background. (US Navy)

The USS *Adder* and its sisters were built and from their commissioning until 1908 taught the Navy much about the submarine and its capabilities. Formed into an operational flotilla in Newport, Rhode Island, in April 1904, the *Adder*, *Moccasin* and *Porpoise* operated out of Newport and Suffolk, New York (Long Island). The *Grampus* and the *Pike* operated out of San Francisco and San Pedro, California. Then in 1908 most were put out of commission. There were two new submarine classes in the water and the Adders were outdated, but not so outdated that some couldn't defend Manila Bay in the Philippines. Admiral George Dewey had said that if the Spanish had possessed one submarine in the bay in 1898, he would not have attacked.

The Adders were stripped down and loaded aboard colliers to make the trip (true "boats"). The *Porpoise* and the *Shark* were first. They went aboard the USS *Caesar* (AC-16). Loading in Newport, the *Caesar* made the trip across the Atlantic, through the Mediterranean, through the Suez Canal and across the Indian Ocean to Manila. Altogether the journey took from April to August 1908. Once the ship made port in Cavite, it offloaded the boats by pushing them overside on skids. Thus the *Porpoise* and the *Shark* were the first US Navy submarines through the Suez Canal and the first to be launched twice. (the *Holland* was launched twice, but only once as a naval ship).

The following year, the *Caesar* made another trip carrying the *Adder* and the *Moccasin*. In late 1912, the USS *Ajax* (AC-15) carried two of the B-Class boats (the *B-2* and *B-3*) to Manila. In 1915, the USS *Hector* (AC-7) took the two west-coast boats, the *Grampus* and the *Pike*, and the *B-1* to Manila. Thus by the end of 1915, the Manila Bay flotilla consisted of six A-Class boats and three B-Class boats. Manila was the first advanced base. These boats escorted ships into and out of Manila during World War I and performed the tasks of a "fleet in being" – that is, one whose presence deters an opponent even if it makes no patrols and sinks none of its foes. After the war, the boats were worn out and used up. By 1918 the S-boats were being built. As large a leap was made in those early 18 years as was made in the period from 1945 to 1963 when the diesel boats were being replaced by nuclear submarines. The Adders were put out of commission for the last time and, in 1922, the Navy

designated them for use as targets. They were towed to a position just outside Manila Bay and sunk over a period of time by destroyer gunfire. As near as we can find out at present, they are still there.

The A-boats were the first in many ways and they showed the way the Submarine Force would be. Ensign Charles Lockwood was most disappointed to be assigned to the USS *Monterey* for duty in submarines. He was told by some of the officers already there that the submarine "would get in your blood and soon either you wouldn't be around or you wouldn't trade the boat for duty on anything else." He discovered within six months that they were right. The man who would become Commander Submarine Force Pacific during the last three years of World War II was never the same again.

The A-Class boats were followed by the B, C and D classes in quick success through the years 1904 to 1908. The E-Class was a slightly modified D-Class with two diesel engines of Vickers design installed. The two boats of this class were the first US submarines to transit the Atlantic unaided and operated in an anti-submarine warfare (ASW) mode during World War I.

Simon Lake's USS *G-1* was laid down in 1909 with many unique elements in its design. Because Lake's concept was to build submarines that were capable of multiple tasks he included items such as wheels to roll across the sea bottom in littoral areas; a diver's lockout chamber so that divers could be employed to cut submarine cables, disable mines and attach limpet mines to surface vessels and drydock caissons; and trainable deck torpedo tubes. Unfortunately, there were many delays and the boat was not completed until 1912.

The Navy was very much concerned about Lake's inability to supply the numbers of submarines needed, meaning that EB would become the sole source supplier. To increase the pool of submarine builders available the Cramp Shipyard of Philadelphia, Pennsylvania, was awarded a contract to build a submarine designed by the Italian maker Laurenti. This boat, the USS *G-4*, was delivered very late and was nearly obsolete when accepted. The design was complex and difficult to build. It didn't lend itself to mass production and had many difficulties in living up to its specifications. The experiment was not repeated.

The year 1911 was early in submarine design and the use to which submarines were to be put was very much in debate. The mainstays of the Submarine Force were the four F-Class, four H-Class and six K-Class boats. It was recognized by the General Board (the Navy body that oversaw acquisition of new ships) that new boats, more modern ones, could be built and were needed. In May the board requested five new boats, to be built to the general design specifications of the existing K-Class, and one submarine tender. However, the Secretary of the Navy, Josephus Daniels, disagreed and did not request any from Congress. Congress, however, being lobbied hard by Isaac Rice of EB and Simon Lake, ordered eight new boats and a tender. The boats purchased were to be K-Class and built to the EB design. Submarine officers requested more modern boats and that Simon Lake designs be used also. Thus, the next class design was split. EB designed an upgraded K-Class and designated it design number EB37G. It was to have the increased hull and bulkhead strength the Submarine Force wanted and other changes. The initial design called for 3in/25cal Mk IX deck guns, but these were not installed initially on the first four of the class. The *L-1*, *L-2*, *L-3* and *L-4* were

The USS *D-2* under way astern possibly in Newport, Rhode Island, in 1914. Note the size difference between this boat and the B and C. All three hatches to the interior are open. The davit just forward of the conning tower fairing is for torpedo reload. (US Navy)

One of the boats designed and built by Simon Lake in his Bridgeport, Connecticut, shipyard, the USS *G-2* lies outboard the USS *G-4*, a Laurenti design built by Cramp in Philadelphia. The boat designs were generally unsuccessful for various reasons and were not repeated. (US Navy)

USS *K-5* under way. Near the bow are the hydrophones of the Y-Tube passive sonar (there were three, but only two are clearly visible here). Just aft the stanchion is the t-shaped C-Tube listening hydrophone. (NARA)

built at the EB facility in Fore River, Massachusetts. They resembled EB's standard expansion on the initial Holland design. The boats were 167ft long and had a beam of 17½ft. They could make 14 knots on the surface using their two NELSECO engines and a maximum of 10½ knots submerged at the one-hour rate. They had four bow torpedo tubes of the small 18in diameter. The boats were divided into five watertight compartments, and had hull strength to maintain a test depth of 200ft. The compartments were the forward torpedo room, forward battery, control, after battery, and the engineering space. EB had dispensed with the standard rotating bow cap closures on the torpedo tubes in favor of the muzzle door-and-shutter arrangement pioneered by Lake. The boats were designed to be coastal vessels and to be used for defense against fleets which might threaten US cities and harbors. Thus, habitability items were not of major concern. There was no air-conditioning and insufficient ventilation. It was assumed that all transits would be on the surface with at least the conning tower hatch open.

Lake was proceeding with the design work for his version of the L-Class but work stopped when he had to declare bankruptcy in 1913. He reorganized his company and commenced work on the *L-5* at his shipyard in Bridgeport, Connecticut. The *L-6* and the *L-7* were started under contract

B Submarines from the earliest time to World War I grew rapidly in size. The right-hand column shows the first four Lake designs. Each of the boats was different in design which was a disadvantage leading to the demise of the Lake company as a submarine supplier. On the left, the Electric Boat designs which built, each in turn, on the original John Holland submarine. By World War I, US submarines were able to transit the Atlantic Ocean. The color schemes changed throughout the period and throughout the boats' lifetimes. However, those shown here were the most common.

1. *Alligator*, 1862
2. *Intelligent Whale*, 1864
3. USS *Holland*, 1900
4. A-Class, 1901
5. B-Class, 1901
6. C-Class, 1905
7. D-Class, 1908

8. F-Class, 1914
9. H-Class, 1913
10. USS *G-1*, 1912
11. USS *G-2*, 1915
12. USS *G-3*, 1915
13. USS *G-4*, 1914

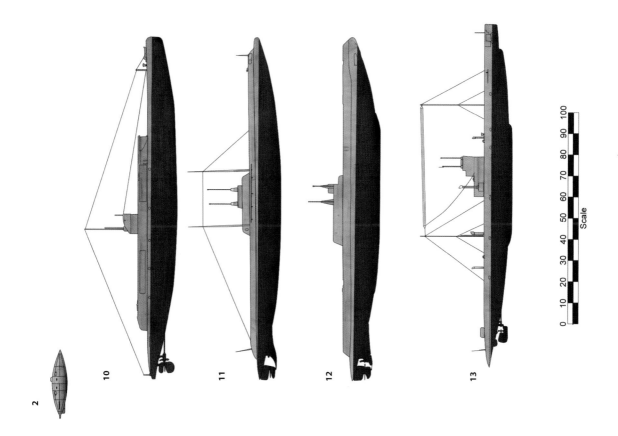

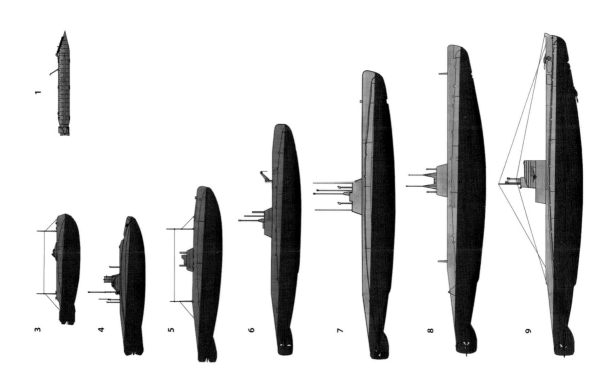

Scale

0 10 20 30 40 50 60 70 80 90 100

The USS *L-8* in drydock at Portsmouth Naval Shipyard, New Hampshire. The submarine was built at this yard using Simon Lake's general plans but had the detail planning done by the government yard. This was a major step away from buying submarines designed by civilian companies and toward the Navy designing and building boats, and civilian companies building to Navy designs. (US Navy)

to Lake at the Crescent Shipyard at Elizabethport, New Jersey. His design was significantly different from that of the EB-built boats. Built on the same dimensions, the Lake boats were designed to dive and maintain depth on an even keel. They also had five watertight compartments: the torpedo room, control, engine room, motor room and tiller room. The superstructure was watertight but was normally flooded when the boat was submerged. It drained when the boat surfaced and helped increase reserve buoyancy, which was a problem with EB boats.

Simon Lake ran into financial problems again and arranged with the Navy to build a boat to his design at a naval shipyard. Josephus Daniels was concerned about the Navy's being dependent on two civilian shipbuilders for its submarines. He said: "I thought that the only way to compel the two private submarine builders to make the best submarines at a reasonable price was to demonstrate they could be built at a Navy Yard." EB would not release the patent rights that would allow a navy yard to build to its design,

The only experimentation in mating aircraft to submarines that actually made it off the drawing board in the US Navy. The diminutive Martin MS-1 could be dismantled and stowed in a canister aft of the conning tower fairing. The experiment was generally unsuccessful but re-emerged in the form of the Loon and Regulus programs using USS *Cusk*, *Carbonero* and *Tunny* after World War II. The canister later was used in one of the first rescue chamber designs. (US Navy)

so Lake was contacted. He was more willing and after some negotiations, the contract for building the *L-8* to a Lake design was awarded to Portsmouth Navy Yard on June 30, 1914. The boat was built in the huge Franklin shiphouse. Many factors delayed construction, but on April 23, 1917, the first submarine built by a naval shipyard was launched. The Navy was, at that time, building a submarine design and shipbuilding base.

By the beginning of World War I, the Navy had developed a certain amount of submarine design expertise and was beginning to understand what it wanted by way of a submarine to meet its expected needs. The desire was for a submarine that could range independently and attack enemy fleets and that could operate with the existing battlefleet. The Atlantic might be a battleground, but even at this early stage the actions of the British and German navies, across the wide Pacific, were being watched closely.

Three prototypes were ordered. The *S-1* would be EB Design 73A and would resemble all the company's past designs. It would incorporate their advantages as well as their flaws. The *S-2* would be a Lake design. This was a more complex design than the EB one, and building a production run of these boats would be problematic as the Lake yard had already undergone one financial reorganization and was operating on a shoestring. The *S-3* was a government design and would be built at a naval shipyard. It would attempt to incorporate what the Navy saw as the best elements of EB, Lake and its own design house's work. In the end, the class was mixed. The Navy built some (the *S-4* to the *S-13*), Lake got a contract to build some boats to the *S-3* design with modifications and built the *S-14* to the *S-17* and the *S-48* to the *S-51*, with the EB design being used for the rest (the *S-18* to the *S-47*). These submarines made up a good part of the US force at the beginning of World War II, albeit being somewhat modified. The construction of the S-Class had far-reaching ramifications in submarine design and acquisition for the US Navy. Prior to World War I the system could be seen as a company approaching the Navy and saying "Here are the submarine designs we have available for you to buy which meet the general specifications you have

The *S-2* slides down the slipway at the Lake Shipyard in Bridgeport, Connecticut, on a cold wet February day in 1919. This was the last of the strictly Lake designs. After a construction contract for some of the end boats in the Navy-designed S series, the Simon Lake submarine construction business went bankrupt in 1924. (US Navy)

USS *M-1* under way. The Navy tried to increase the size of the submarine to allow for larger and more powerful engines to increase speed to a point where the submarine could keep up with the battlefleet. The increase in size was seen in the T-Class and the M-Class. Unfortunately these boats, although faster, were not fast enough and with the size increase, other problems appeared. The boats were not very maneuverable and slow in diving, and unwieldy and slow when submerged. (US Navy SFLM)

published." The Navy, having little or no design capability or expertise, would be forced to choose from what was being offered. If only one company made offers a single source monopoly might soon develop; this was good for the company concerned, but not so good for the Navy. With the building of the *L-8* at Portsmouth Navy Yard and the design and development work on the M, T, and S classes, the Navy gained enough design experience to change the system of acquisition. Now the Navy went to the company and said in effect: "Here is the submarine design we want you to build. You and other companies may bid on contracts to build this design and you may be in competition with the cost and capabilities of producing submarines of this design at naval shipyards." It was not a perfect system, but it suited the production that would be needed during the run-up to World War II and during that war's intense production schedules.

One consequence was the demise of the Lake company. Prior to the S-Class, the design and building of the L, N, O and R classes was split between the Electric Boat Company and the Lake Torpedo Boat Company. Thus the classes had several boats built to each company's design. The Lake boats were deemed less useful than the EB designs and Lake's company had a history of being underfunded and poorly managed. On the plus side for Lake was his exclusive contract with Busch-Sulzer which made engines which were more reliable and with better histories than the EB-built NELSECO engines. After World War I, the Navy evaluated the Lake, EB and its own designs and production capabilities. The Lake Torpedo Boat Company came up short in the evaluation and the Navy was forced to make the difficult choice between continuing to contract Lake or building up its own production potential to rival EB's. It chose the latter. The lack of postwar

C Along with the increase in size and complexity of the submarine itself, the propulsion train was the focus of intense engineering study. The *Holland*'s train (**1**) was simple but included all the elements needed for a successful submarine. That being some type of engine driving the screw propeller and a dynamo. The dynamo was used to charge the battery that supplied energy for submerged running. The K-Class (**2**) used heavy oil (diesel engine) rather than gasoline which was much safer. The shaft got longer and had auxiliary equipment either directly on the shaft or belt (or chain) driven from the shaft. The S-Class shaft (**3**) was so long that it ran into a serious torsional vibration problem that led to cracked and broken crank shafts and other issues. The answer to this long shaft issue was to decouple the diesel engine completely from driving the main shaft. The propeller was driven by electric motors which didn't have the vibration issue, as seen, for example, in the propulsion train of the later Gato Class submarines (**4**).

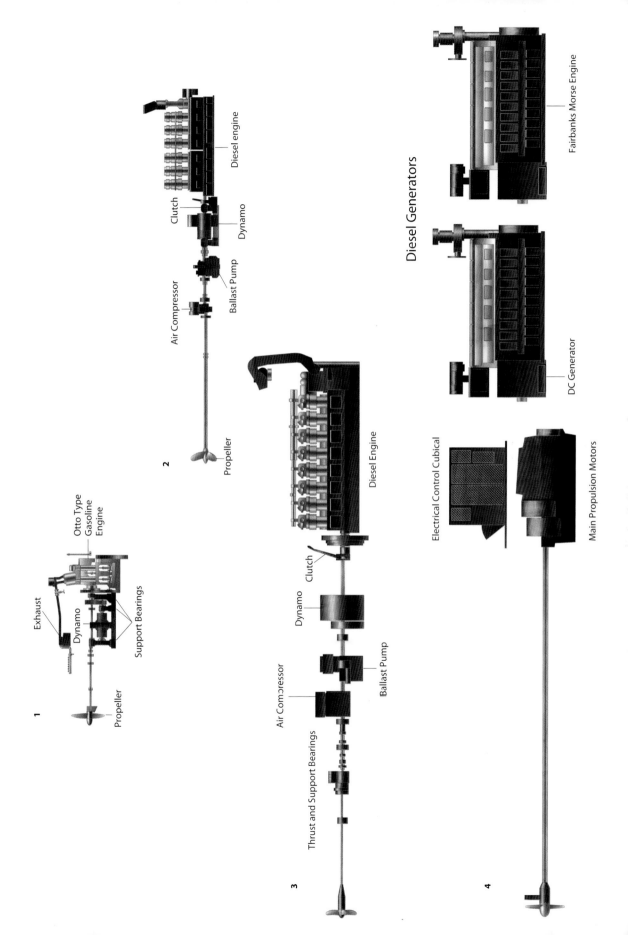

1

Exhaust

Otto Type Gasoline Engine

Dynamo

Support Bearings

Propeller

2

Diesel engine

Clutch

Dynamo

Ballast Pump

Air Compressor

Propeller

3

Diesel Engine

Clutch

Dynamo

Ballast Pump

Air Compressor

Thrust and Support Bearings

4

Diesel Generators

Fairbanks Morse Engine

DC Generator

Electrical Control Cubical

Main Propulsion Motors

The forward starboard corner of the control room on USS *M-1*. It appears that some of the wiring is not yet properly installed or some test is being conducted. The levers to the right operate Kingston valves which allow water into the ballast tanks. The helm wheel is to the left and above it is the access hatch to the conning tower. (US Navy SFLM)

submarine contracts hastened the demise of the Lake Torpedo Boat Company and in 1924 it closed its doors for good.

EB weathered the lack of submarine contracts and the Great Depression by building other ships and even submarines for Peru (modified R-Class boats). Its diversity and capabilities allowed it to successfully bid for contracts starting again in 1931 with what would be the USS *Dolphin* (*V-9*) and it subsequently became a major force in submarine building in the US, a role it maintains to this day.

In the years between the world wars submarine technology bridged the gap from a weapons system for harbor and coastal defense to one that could range over all the world's oceans and threaten enemy convoys and fleets wherever found. The US Navy wrote detailed design specifications for its new submarines. A first attempt at a fleet submarine in the US Navy was the T-Class of 1916. These boats had four diesel engines to provide the required horsepower to drive the 268ft-long hull at the designed 20 knots. Two engines each were connected in tandem on each shaft. This proved too complex to be reliable. Another attempt at the large submarine design was the first three boats of what was loosely termed the V-Class. Designed in 1920, these boats split the diesel plant so that two engines drove electric generators and were situated forward of the control room. Two other engines were situated aft in the standard direct-drive configuration, one to each shaft. These boats had grown to over 2,000 tons and 330ft in length. They proved to be unhandy in diving and maneuvering. Even in later life, converted to cargo carriers, the three were generally considered unsuccessful. Throughout the 1920s the submarine design community, which consisted of constructors, submarine commanders and engineers, worked to develop, build and test new designs in an atmosphere of disarmament. This work resulted in several designs which, when built, were to become the remainder of the V-Class. The *Argonaut*, or *V-4*, was built as a minelayer capable of carrying 60 Mk XI mines and laying these through two 40in-diameter tubes in the stern. Two large cruiser submarines, the *Nautilus* and the *Narwhal*, were designated the *V-5* and the *V-6*. These were very similar to the *Argonaut*

Submarines of EB and Lake design alongside in New London, Connecticut, about 1918. The EB-designed boat is inboard. Above the fairwater is the 'chariot' bridge. On the after deck the engine room hatch is open. The men in the punt aft are most likely painting the boat, a task performed by the author in similar conditions at the same pier on a submarine some 45 years later. Next outboard is a Lake boat. The superstructure indicates it is likely to be the *G-1*. (US Navy)

but without the minelaying tubes. All three of these (the *V-4*, *V-5* and *V-6*) carried the largest deck guns of any US submarine, the 6in/53cal Mk XII Mod 2. The boats were plagued by early engine reliability problems and underwent engine replacements early in World War I. The *Dolphin*, or *V-7*, was to be a bit smaller and less expensive than the six large boats that preceded it. It had a rearranged tankage and hull framing, and its internal layout was the forerunner of the standard model of fleet submarine. The last two of the V-Class, the *Cachalot* and the *Cuttlefish*, started the trend towards welding. EB, which built the *Cuttlefish*, used extensive welding throughout the period, while Portsmouth Navy Yard retained riveting as the structural fastening method for the *Cachalot*. The design trend, although slowed during the depression years, culminated in the design and construction of the famed Gato and Balao Classes which wreaked havoc in the Pacific during World War II.

A bow view of the USS *Pike* being painted in San Diego. The bow cap is clearly shown. It looks somewhat like the beak on a cuttlefish. Atop the superstructure is the helm wheel, a platform with railing that would be the forerunner of the bridge on later submarines. (US Navy)

THE TECHNOLOGY

Basic design
US submarine design and construction had taken two distinct paths, but these converged in the 1930s as the US government took over the design and applied its own designs to the acquisition process. Initially, private companies took the general specifications issued by the Navy and applied these to their own "in house" design processes. The general specifications covered items such as speed, displacement, armament

and operational range. How the specifications were met was entirely the decision of the private company's designers. The design or designs generated were then presented to the Navy and contracts for the construction of vessels written. This process was used not only for submarines but for surface vessels as well.

As mentioned earlier, two companies were equipped to vie for the government contracts to build submarines. First was the Holland Torpedo Boat Company which, run by Isaac Rice, held the patent rights for the innovations developed by John Holland. This became the Electric Boat Company (EB). The other submarine builder was the Lake Torpedo Boat Company. Started and run by Simon Lake, its thrust was to build military submarines and commercial marine salvage devices.

Basic form

The two major builders constructed submarines with two different and wholly distinct design elements that were based on their patent holdings and differing thoughts on submarine operation. From 1900 to 1920 Holland/EB-designed hull form remained relatively constant. Such boats are easily identified by their general characteristics. The "Holland" hull was a "body of revolution" with each hull station being a circle with their centers in a straight line. Starting at the bow, the design used a rotating bow cap to close the muzzles of the torpedo tubes.

With two tubes this meant that both were either closed or both were open and flooded for firing. Therefore, one tube could not be reloaded while the other was ready for firing. With four tubes, the cap concept meant that two tubes could be open to sea for firing at a time while the other two tubes' muzzles were closed. This limitation was overcome with the L-Class which used muzzle doors and shutters. The superstructure was narrow and free-flooding.

The conning tower was a vertical cylinder which was faired for a bit less drag and in later boats was topped by a "chariot" bridge. The aft portion of the superstructure formed a skeg which helped support the upper section of the rudder. The rudder and stern planes were in a cruciform arrangement about the ship's longitudinal centerline.

Propulsion shafting was placed along the centerline until the C-Class. It was parallel to the centerline on each side thereafter. The hull design with direct drive from the engines required a slight upward angle on the main shafts as the boats got larger and longer. The submarine submerged by taking water into the ballast tanks through a keel duct until they were full. Fine-tuning of the buoyancy was performed by use of a "compensating tank." Depth control was by use of the stern planes which, like elevators on an aircraft, changed the angle of the boat in the water – if an up angle the boat rose toward the surface and if a down angle it dove deeper. This constant change of angle and depth was termed "porpoising" and was an adequate method of control given the slow speed of the boat. The EB designs didn't change in basic form from the A-Class of 1900 to the S-Class of 1916, which formed the entire run of EB designs, except for increasing length, beam, displacement and internal structures such as bulkheads.

Simon Lake, of the Lake Torpedo Boat Company, designed his submarines to submerge and operate submerged on an even keel. The hull design involved a circular pressure hull with the centers of each circle on a gentle U-shaped curve upward at the ends. The rudder and stern planes were mounted in structures below the stern in a manner resembling a surface-ship design. Hydroplanes were mounted along the beam to control depth. Depth changes were to be on an even keel using the planes to drive the boat up and down without angle change. Where the EB designs had a free-flooding

The stern of *N-1*. The man in the foreground is standing just inboard the port propulsion shaft. The propeller is not yet installed. His arm is resting on the upper rudder support. Along his left knee is the reach rod lever for the stern planes which are just below his feet. (US Navy SFLM)

This image of the *G-2* shows some of the Lake design elements such as the oval torpedo loading hatch and the closed superstructure. There were valves which opened to allow the superstructure to flood on diving. Submerged, the Lake boats did not change depth by taking an up or down angle but 'planed' up and down on an even keel using hydroplanes along the hull. (US Navy)

The launch of *S-10*. Workmen are knocking out the wedges holding the boat in place. At the right is the starboard bow plane and fender rail. Just above the forward end of the anti-rolling keel is the Fessenden oscillator. This electromagnetic sound projector superseded the signaling bell and was the forerunner of the active sonar transmitter. (US Navy)

superstructure (casing) the Lake design had a superstructure that was partially watertight and acted as a buoyancy element for surface operation (aiding sea keeping). In keeping with Lake's concepts of strategic and tactical submarine use, his first design accepted by the Navy (the USS *G-1*) had wheels near the keel and a diver lockout chamber. He felt the submarine was not only a torpedo-firing platform but could also be used to cut communication cables, clear minefields, lay mines and perform other useful underwater work. The boats had several internal watertight bulkheads which were curved, making them difficult to fabricate. These and other innovations such as trainable superstructure-mounted torpedo tubes made his boats more complex and less suited to mass production.

Engines

Submarines have relied on engines fueled by petroleum products – gasoline, paraffin, and both light and heavy oils – to provide energy for propulsion on the surface and while submerged if using a snorkel.

Gasoline engines were used early in submarine development because they were the only engines available that were light enough, and small enough to fit in existing hulls. Unlike the gasoline engines in automobiles and trucks today, these were bulky units with bolt-up and threaded connections and fittings that would loosen and leak. The engines were commercially built by Otto of Philadelphia; EB at the Fore River shipyard (these were Craig-designed engines); White and Middleton (for Lake boats) in Springfield, Ohio; and, for the Laurenti-designed *G-4*, Fiat of Italy.

The shift to diesel engines was not without controversy. Gasoline engines, although dangerous, were more reliable than the early diesel ones available. EB wanted to install diesel engines built by its new partner Vickers. However, the Navy Bureau of Engineering wanted to stay with gasoline engines. In the end, EB's proposal for two boats with diesel engines, the E-Class (which was essentially a D-Class with diesel engines), and the remainder of the D-Class with gasoline ones, won the day. The two E-Class boats would prove reliable and safe enough to turn the corner from gasoline-powered submarines to diesel-powered submarines.

Engine design and construction was fraught with difficulties. Material strength and torsional vibration were serious stumbling blocks. Even though theoretical solutions to these issues had been proposed and some practical

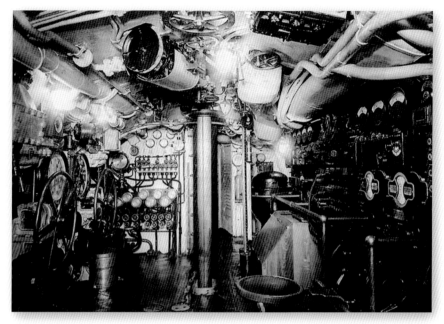

The control room of the ill-fated *S-4*. On the left are the hand operators for the bow and stern planes. On the right is the open-front electrical switchboard with the protective railings. Just forward of the switchboard is the Sperry gyrocompass. This boat sank off Cape Cod after a collision with the Coast Guard cutter *Paulding*. Although the wreck was in only 100ft of water, the crew that had survived in the torpedo room could not be rescued and perished. This disaster and the loss of the *S-51* (rammed by a merchant ship in 1925) led directly to the adoption of escape facilities in submarines and methods of fixing the position of a sunken submarine. (US Navy)

knowledge had been gained with steam engines, the higher speeds, higher cylinder pressures, temperatures, and the effect of multiple cylinders in gasoline and diesel engines meant that design practice could not rise to the challenge for some time. The main problem can be viewed as three interconnecting issues. First, the temperatures and pressures necessary to make Dr Rudolf Diesel's concept a reality tested material strength and property design. Cylinders overheated and cracked. Intake and exhaust valves burned out and broke, frequently falling into the cylinder and wrecking it and the piston. Then the force developed by the expanding gas in the cylinder bent connecting rods. The repetitive impact force of the piston, transmitted to the crankshaft, tended to distort a lightly built support structure. This distortion was more pronounced in a submarine hull than on a factory test stand because of the relatively lighter hull structure. There was then the

The Electric Boat Company owned the New London Ship and Engine Company (NELSECO) which built engines at first using a Vickers license then to EB's own design. This is a six-cylinder four-cycle NELSECO engine of the type used in EB submarines from the E Class through the S Class. The NELSECO site in Groton, Connecticut, is the present site of the Electric Boat Division of General Dynamics. (US Navy)

The engine room of an N-Class boat looking forward. Main motors are in the foreground right and left with the engines ahead of them. The levers on quadrants just aft the engines are part of the engine controls. The door in the middle leads to the battery compartment. (US Navy)

problem of torsional vibration, seen in the entire drive train, from the engine's crankshaft to the propeller. The crankshaft was connected by a short shaft to a manual clutch. From the clutch a shaft ran through the armature of a DC dynamo to another clutch. From this second clutch the shaft ran further aft through a thrust bearing and the pressure hull packing (shaft seal) to the propeller. As the boats got larger, this shaft arrangement got longer and torsional vibration problems became more prevalent. A large part of the problem was that the engines operated at speeds at, or very near, the resonant frequency of the propulsion train or one of its harmonics. At the resonant frequency, the forcing motion would enhance the vibration amplitude. The variations in the force caused by the piston motion (due to cylinder firing) results in a torsional (twisting) vibration in the propulsion train which caused the crankshaft or propulsion shaft to crack, and in some cases break.

In the switch to diesel engines, EB used the four-cycle diesels built under the Vickers license at EB's Fore River plant. However, in 1909 the US Navy (after several collisions and near-disasters because of lack of maneuverability) required that the submarine builders use reversible engines. Before this change the submarine had to make a time-consuming propulsion train configuration change to go from ahead to astern. In ahead, the engine drove the propeller directly via the propulsion shaft. In this shaft train were two

D Weapons used on early submarines were the automobile torpedo such as the Whitehead Mk II (**1**) shown here. These torpedos evolved in their range and, during the interwar years, in their ability to change course. Deck guns started out as the 3"/25cal Mark IX (**2**) which had a limited range and punch. After World War I, submarines were equipped with guns similar to the 4"/50 (**3**). This gun was a mainstay weapon throughout World War II until it was finally replaced by the 5"/25cal.

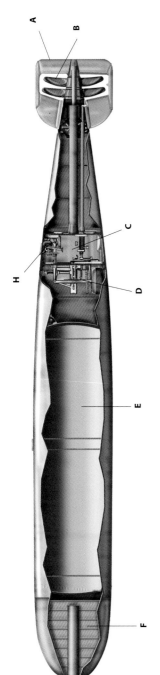

1

A Rudder
B Contra-rotating propellers
C Air Motor
D Angle sensing mechanism

E Air flask
F Wet guncotton warhead
G Fuse enabling propeller
H Depth sensing mechanism

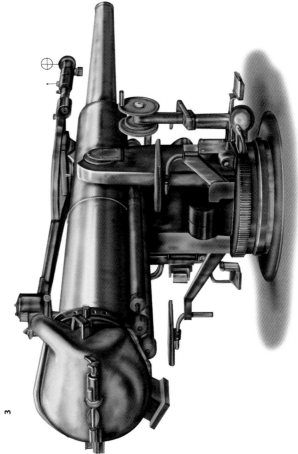

3

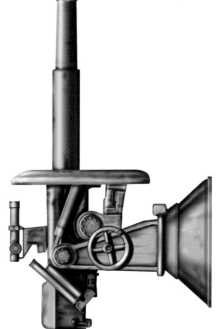

2

clutches, one on each side of the electric dynamo. To go astern, the engine had to be stopped, the clutch between the engine and the dynamo opened and the shaft started astern on the dynamo acting as a motor. This operation could take up to two minutes. This was clearly an unacceptable time lag for operating in confined water. Thus the Navy made the move to requiring reversible engines. This meant that EB had to dispense with the Vickers engine and go with that built by MAN (Maschinenfabrik Augsburg-Nürnberg AG). EB then established the New London Ship and Engine Company (NELSECO) in Groton, Connecticut. These engines – the Vickers to some extent and especially the MAN designs – suffered from a vibration problem that would plague EB and the Navy until submarine design went to all-diesel-electric engines.

Lake used White and Middleton gasoline engines at first, then in the shift to diesel entered into an exclusive contract to use Busch-Sulzer two-cycle engines. These engines were robust and gave good service. As the boats got larger the engines got larger but suffered little of the torsional vibration problems of the MAN or NELSECO engines.

By 1928 the concept of diesel-electric was gaining favor as there was a desire to use larger engines with more power. However, to drive even longer shafts directly was becoming more difficult. Ganging engines on a common shaft was tried but was not successful. Diesel-electric drive simply meant that the engine was close-coupled to an electric generator. The unit was more compact and less prone to the problems of long-shafted direct drive. The output of the generator then was connected through a switchboard to either the battery for charging or main propulsion motors for driving the propellers, or both. The diving times were shortened (which was desirable in light of the threat of aircraft attacks) as the time to shift from engine-provided electrical power to battery-supplied power was a matter of shifting a few (albeit robust) switches. The engines could be run at economical speeds outside the resonant-frequency areas. Three engine

The battery and berthing compartment of an L-Class boat, looking aft. The watertight door to the control room is seen on the left side of the bulkhead while battery ventilation blower controls are on the right. Mattresses are seen in the upper right and left on the bunks which are triced up. The large cylinder in the center is the housing for the 3in/25cal Mk IX deck gun. This, obstruction, plus other problems, caused the Navy to seek a better deck gun. (US Navy SFLM)

The Lake-designed *G-1* in drydock. The openings in the side of the superstructure are for trainable deck-mounted torpedo tubes. The two tall masts fore and aft are for mounting the radio antenna. Aft of the main superstructure is a 'clamshell' opening that gives access to the aft pressure hull. This feature was revived in the superstructure associated with the Navy' GUPPY III development program nearly 60 years later. (US Navy)

manufacturers obtained contracts to build diesel-electric engines: Fairbanks Morse (FM), Winton (which became Cleveland Diesel then General Motors, or GM) and Hoover, Oven, Rentscheler (HOR). The first two were very successful and provided the engines for the fleet submarines of World War II and beyond. FM still supplies emergency diesel generators for the US Submarine Force today.

Batteries

The design of electric storage batteries remained relatively stable during this entire period. The ratio of energy capacity to weight for batteries is generally poor but until the advent of nuclear propulsion and some air-independent propulsion systems there was no viable alternative for submerged operation. The basic form of the lead acid storage battery has remained unchanged in all but technical details from the late 19th century to today.

EB used Isaac Rice's Electric Storage Battery Company's cells (which some say was the impetus for Rice to get into the submarine business in the first place). This company became the Exide Corporation. The batteries were basically plates of pure lead and lead oxide mounted on a supporting grid forming a plate which was then suspended in a solution of sulfuric acid. The individual plates were separated by insulating glass-fiber mats and connected in series on their upper ends to form cells of a common number of plates. The cells were then connected in series to provide a useful voltage range. Each cell was a steel box lined with hard rubber on the inside and outside. It was open-topped to allow access to the cells for monitoring, refilling the electrolyte and maintenance. Later the cells were made of hard rubber only (as the steel was prone to corrosion when the hard rubber cracked) and completely enclosed. This arrangement was very tender even when each cell was properly supported and wedged but overall resulted in fewer problems with leaking electrolyte. It is this electrolyte leakage and its attendant corrosion that most likely contributed to the structure failures that caused

Loading a torpedo into *A-2*. Two things are of particular interest in this photo. First, the torpedo is being loaded aft-end first without the use of a skid to rest it on while being lowered into the boat. Second is the hatch arrangement common to early submarines. (US Navy SFLM)

the loss of the USS *F-4*. In the interwar period the cell wall construction was changed to a double-wall system, called the Sargo cell, in which a layer of soft rubber was placed in the space between the cell walls. The design resembles that of older automobile safety glass.

Lake used batteries made by the Gould Corporation which were very much like the Exide Corporation's battery. The only other type used was an Edison battery of nickel hydrate and iron oxide. This was tried in the *E-2* but it was unsuccessful as it generated inordinate amounts of hydrogen and oxygen – in fact, the battery in the *E-2* blew up.

Armament

Only two types of deck gun were used on US submarines during this period. The first was the diminutive 3in/23cal Mk IX. It fired a projectile of about 13lb up to about 4½ miles. Used in submarines it had no remote fire-control

E Post-World War I, submarine designs continued to increase in size and capability. The EB designs grew along the lines of the original Holland work, while the Lake yard was issued contracts that were offshoots of EB's class contracts. These led to splitting the classes into EB and Lake boats. Note, for example, the differences between the Lake and EB O-Classes. The Navy took over submarine design with the S-Class. This shift resulted in the designs used through World War II and today.

1. K-Class, 1912
2. L-Class (EB), 1916
3. O-Class (EB), 1918
4. R-Class, (EB), 1919
5. *S-1* (EB), 1920
6. *S-3* (Navy), 1919
7. *S-42* (EB), early World War II configuration

8. M-Class, 1918
9. L-Class (Lake) 1916
10. O-Class (Lake), 1918
11. R-Class (Lake), 1919
12. *S-2* (Lake), 1920
13. *S-48*, 1939

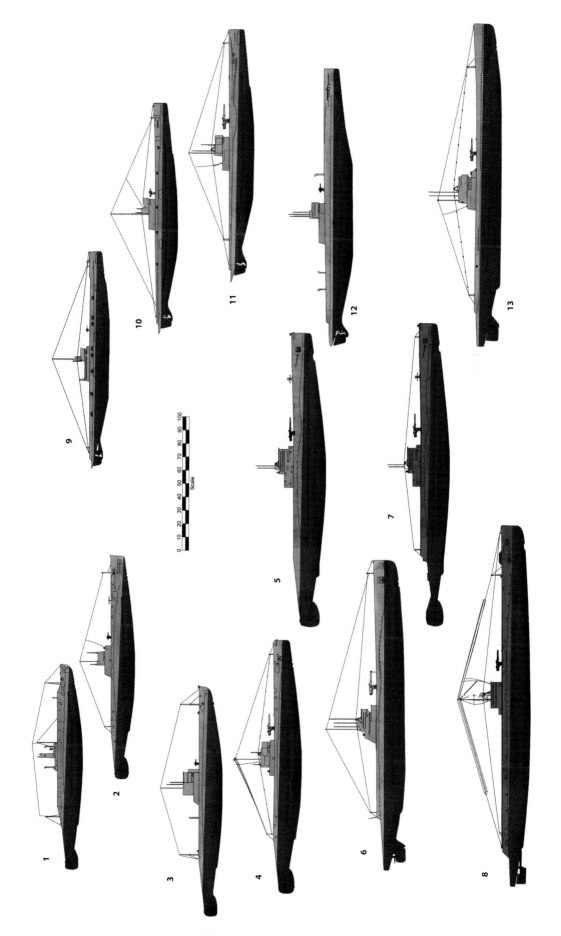

1

2

3

4

5

6

7

8

9

10

11

12

13

0 10 20 30 40 50 60 70 80 90 100

Scale

system and was used in line of sight only. The mount was retractable in that the barrel assembly could be elevated to 90 degrees and the whole thing lowered into a containment cylinder.

What appears to be a splinter shield was the watertight cover that fitted snugly to the top of the containment. The gun's drawbacks were that it had a fairly short range and it was prone to retracting when fired or at other inopportune times. Thus one kept ones toes away from the containment rim.

The second type of deck gun was the 4in/50cal. The gun was of a standard make and model used on destroyers. It was a reliable weapon and lasted through much of World War II, being a replacement for the fleet submarine's 3in/50cal and itself being replaced by the 5in/25cal for submarine use.

Torpedoes evolved throughout this period. The Whitehead Mk II was a straight-running torpedo manufactured by the E. W. Bliss Company. It was about 15ft long and 18in in diameter, thus dictating the size of the torpedo tubes on submarines. It had a range of about 800yd at over 25 knots and carried an explosive charge of 118lb. Gun-cotton was the explosive of choice until about 1911 when this was replaced by trinitrotoluene or TNT. This in turn was replaced by torpex in about 1930. The 18in-diameter torpedo tube was superseded by the 21in torpedo tube with the EB R-Class. The torpedoes used in the smaller tube, and thus prior to the R-Class, were improved versions of the Mk II and culminated in the Bliss-Levitt Mk VII which was propelled by a steam turbine system. This system was in use throughout World War II with the classic Mk XIV torpedo. The larger tube took the Mk X. Introduced during World War I, this torpedo could carry an explosive warhead of nearly 500lb out to a distance of 3,500yd at 36 knots. Electric torpedoes were experimented with during World War I, but unsuccessfully.

Three C-class submarines in a nest (tied up alongside one another) with the outboard boat having a torpedo swung aboard using the boat's portable kingpost davit arrangement. Note that the photo nicely illustrates naval technological transition elements, with a three-masted sail-equipped vessel in the right background and an armored cruiser – the outboard of the two vessels aft of the submarines. Inboard the cruiser is another three-masted vessel with its topmasts down. (US Navy)

Radio

Naval use of radio was well recognized and the technology was used extensively, starting in the first decade of the 20th century. Early transmitters were of the spark gap type but they were replaced by continuous-wave transmitters using the Poulsen arc. Receivers were of the crystal type with various elements being tried. Eventually, heterodyning and beat frequency oscillators were invented and their efficiency was so improved that by World War I most submarines were equipped with relatively low-powered transmitters (about 1kW) and receiver sets that could communicate in the low meter bands to a range of about 30 nautical miles. One major problem for submarines was the antenna. Early ones were long wire antennae which needed to be erected on removable masts. This took time and delayed a submarine's diving. The Bureau of Engineering devised an antenna which included a pair of wires running fore and aft like the mine- and net-clearing "jumping wires." By 1930 a submarine could receive broadcasts while submerged using a short-wire antenna on the periscope or a retractable longer mast-mounted antenna.

Sonar

Experiments on signaling through water had been made in the late 1800s using bells. Submarines in the first decade of the 20th century signaled to each other using bells mounted inverted on the deck with clappers operated from within by air. Dr Reginald Fessenden expanded on this concept by devising an electromagnetic oscillator that worked in water to send messages via code in a manner similar to radio communication, albeit with a much slower data rate. Listening to the sounds was by means of suitably enclosed microphones lowered into the water or mounted on the hull. By World War I these concepts

On the foredeck just above the bow planes are the three arms of the K-Tube sonar – a set of three hydrophones mounted in a streamlined structure. The circular duct-like structure on the upper stem is a towing fairlead. These two boats have the 3in/25cal Mk IX, the barrel of which sticks up from the deck just forward of the conning tower fairing. (US Navy)

The *F-4* and the pontoons used to raise it lie in a floating drydock in Pearl Harbor, Hawaii. Although the collapsed section is clearly visible, the cause of the sinking was the influx of water through an acid-weakened hull plate which caused the boat to become heavy so that the crew could not regain depth control. (US Navy SFLM)

had been developed into active and passive systems (involving the sending of acoustic signals into the water and listening for noises in the water, respectively). Sending was by means of Fessenden oscillators mounted on either side of the bow below the waterline, and listening was by means of microphones. The early systems of microphones (now called hydrophones) were the Coolidge (C-Tube) which used rubber spheres on the ends of the arms of a T-shaped pipe. These were developed into the SC sonar which looked similar but was permanently mounted on the submarine deck. Further experiments resulted in a small fixed array (the K-Tube). Prior to World War I, US submarines were equipped with signaling bells. During the war most K, L, and N boats had K-Tube sonar receivers. In the immediate postwar years the suite for submarines was somewhat standardized, with most boats having the Fessenden oscillator and the MB receiver/detector (a modified version of the K-Tube which used signal waveform interference to localize the sound). The oscillator was superseded by the "supersonic" oscillator which produced a sound in the range just above that which the human ear can hear. The signal allowed for finer detection angles. The MB receiver group of hull-mounted microphones gave way in the late 1920s to in-water

F On December 17, 1917, off La Jolla, California, the USS *F-3* was coming slowly about and was crossing 310° when, at about 1912hrs, its lookouts and officer of the deck (OOD) sighted the masthead and port running light of another ship closing at a combined speed of nearly 20 knots. The OOD screamed for the *F-3*'s helmsman to put the rudder hard over to turn faster to starboard and for the engines to be reversed. The other ship was crossing *F-3*'s bow from starboard to port. The other ship was the *F-1*, running to the south on 165°. Seeing the lights of the *F-3* looming out of the fog, the *F-1*'s skipper tried to come to starboard. The combination of efforts was too slow to do anything but make the collision worse by placing the ships at more of a right angle. The resulting collision was deadly.

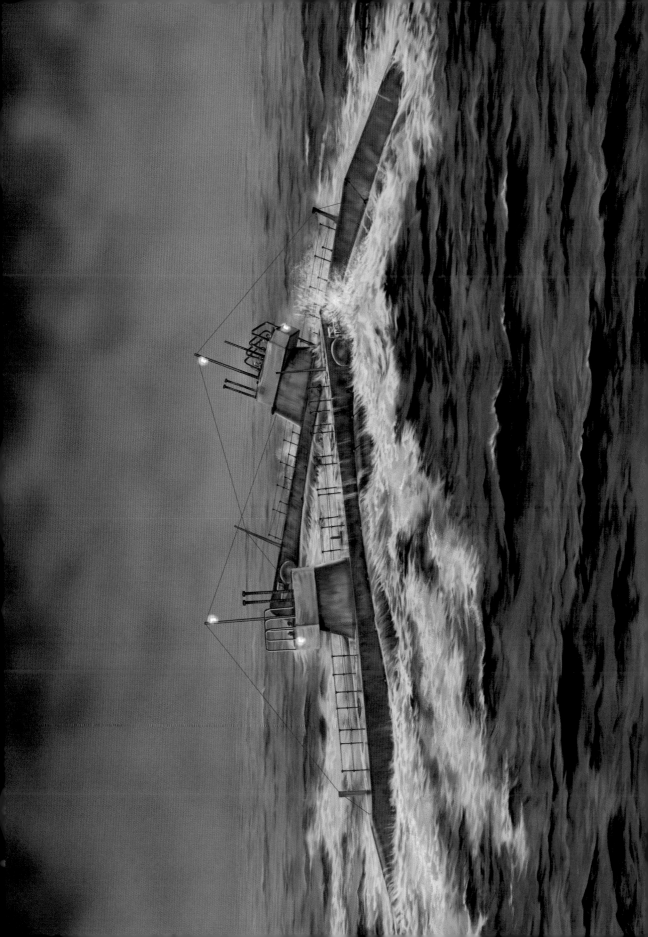

hydrophones as part of an external active/passive oscillator system (now called a projector system) which was initially mounted on the deck, but later lowered from the underside of the submarine when in use.

THE NAMING OF SUBMARINES

The names given to submarines were at the discretion of the builder but came under the general category of names of things that stung, fish, or other "denizens of the deep", until November 11, 1911. On that date, the names of the submarines then in existence were changed to a letter/number combination that indicated the class designation and the position of the boat within the class. Thus, for example, the USS *Grampus* became the USS *A-3*. Some boats had the name-change after they were commissioned, some while in building before commissioning and some while in building before they were ever christened (at launch). The *Holland*'s name was not changed. The A through D classes had their name changed while they were in commission. The *G-1*'s name was changed after launching but before it was commissioned. The E-Class, F-Class, *G-2*, *G-3*, *G-4* and *H-1* thorough *H-3* had the change made while being built but before launching and the K-Class had names changed after being ordered but before laying down. The T-Class also had name changes. The first boat started out as the *AA-1* then in 1920 became the *SF-1*. In October 1920, after a second look at the reclassification scheme, the name was changed to the *T-1*. The others in the class, the *AA-2* and the *AA-3*, had similar changes.

General Order 541 of July 17, 1920, set forth the hull number and type letter designation for US naval ships. There were six standard double-letter designators for submarines. For submarines the following definitions were made: submarine, first line – SS; submarine, second line – OSS; fleet submarine, first line – SF; fleet submarine, second line – OSF; cruiser submarine – SC; minelaying submarine – SM. The double letter designator is not an acronym but is used to differentiate the designators from the practice in most other navies of using single letters as type designators. In the period since then, several other type designators have been added and some deleted. Submarine hull numbers were backdated from 1920 to include submarines accepted into the Navy after 1900. One error was made and the USS *G-1* for a time used the hull number 19½. No submarine in commission from 1900 to July 1920 carried a hull number designation during its commissioned lifetime. Submarine hull numbers start with "1" and go to (at present) 783. They are not consecutive as named but are generally consecutive as ordered. Several gaps occur when groups of contracts or single contracts are cancelled. A notable exception is the group *SSN-21* to *SSN-23*.

OPERATIONS

Disaster 1: The USS *F-4*

Honolulu, Hawaii, is a wonderfully warm and sunny place. The USS *F-4* was on a routine training trip just outside the harbor on March 25, 1915. It started its trim dive about a mile south of Sand Island where the water shelves off from 400ft to several thousand feet in the space of a mile or so. As the boat dove below a depth that its periscope could peek above the water, trouble started. A dull pop was heard and a shudder in air pressure was felt. Soon the boat was heavy and the crew started to pump from the compensating tank into the sea. The boat became still heavier and the order was given to blow the main ballast tanks dry with high-pressure air. However, instead of blowing the water out of the ballast tanks, the air blew into the boat's interior because the upper portion of the ballast tank, right under the battery, had ruptured. The boat's fate was sealed. It dropped below its safe operating depth limit in a few minutes and then below its designed maximum hull strength depth (crush depth). The pressure hull in the torpedo room failed catastrophically and all 21 crewmembers died. The boat hit the bottom in nearly 400ft of water. It was the first time the US Navy had lost a submarine and its crew. Great efforts were made to reach the ship and rescue the crew, but because of the depth of water there was no hope. The wreck was finally raised the next year. Investigation determined that the cause of the sinking was a structural failure in the forward battery well due to acid leakage from the batteries. The sulfuric acid electrolyte had, over a period of time, caused heavy corrosion of rivets on tank seams which, in their weakened state, failed and caused the flooding of the ship. The submarine's remains were eventually placed in a deep trench buried by new wharf construction off the north side of the submarine base at Pearl Harbor, where it still resides today.

Disaster 2: The USS *F-1*

The distance from San Pedro Bay to La Jolla in California is roughly 75 nautical miles. A course connecting Point Fermin, the southern point of the Palos Verdes Hills, with Point Loma is 142°T. The reciprocal then would be 322°T. To transit between these two points, one would go south on 142° and to come back one would steer 322°. In a smooth sea the F-Class submarine could make the trip

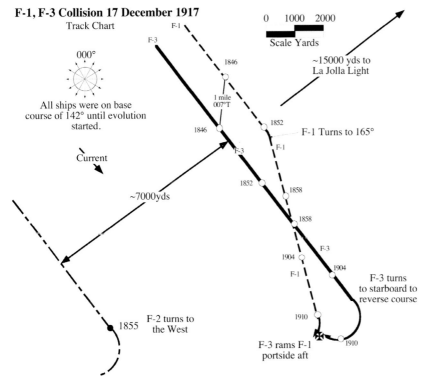

F-1, F-3 Collision 17 December 1917
Track Chart

0   1000   2000
Scale Yards

000°

All ships were on base course of 142° until evolution started.

Current

~7000yds

1846

1 mile 007°T

1846

1852

~15000 yds to La Jolla Light

1852

1858

F-1 Turns to 165°

1858

1904

1904

F-3 turns to starboard to reverse course

1910

F-3 rams F-1 portside aft

1910

1855   F-2 turns to the West

Compiled from written sources at Submarine Force Library and Museum   J.L.Christley USN(ret)

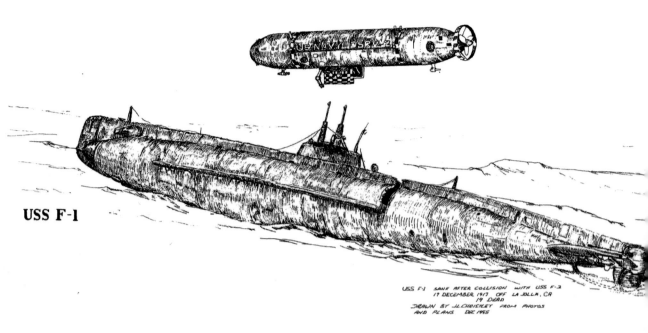

USS F-1

USS F-1 SANK AFTER COLLISION WITH USS F-3
17 DECEMBER 1917 OFF LA JOLLA, CA
19 DEAD
DRAWN BY J.L.CHRISTLEY FROM PHOTOS
AND PLANS. DEC 1995

An artist's impression of a deep submergence rescue vessel hovering over the wreck of the USS *F-1* off the coast of California. The DSRV-2 located and photographed the wreck in 1980. The boat sank after a collision with the USS *F-1* in December 1917. (Author's Collection)

in about eight hours at just less than 10 knots. Naval instructions require that ships perform an engineering test to determine both the stamina of a ship and its capabilities. Both must be known in order to plan strategy. The test for submarines was to run at a constant standard speed for 48 hours, which would indicate how far the ship could go in the requisite time. Slowing or stopping for repairs would count against the ship's performance and reflect poorly on the ship and crew. The best a ship could do, then, was to maintain a constant, fairly high, speed for the entire time. To do a 48-hour engineering test would require six trips for the F-Class boats, three trips south from San Pedro toward San Diego and three back to the north.

G By January of 1918, the US Navy had deployed submarines along the east coast of the US on ASW patrols looking for German submarines. The greatest danger they faced, however, was from the ships in convoy and their escorts. For example, the USS *O-6*, patrolling out of Cold Spring Inlet, New Jersey, was trailing a convoy from about two miles astern. The submarine was ordered to follow the convoy and be on the lookout for U-boats lurking about and make a stern approach on any found. The ship's log then notes:

> At 3.05 p.m. the last ship fired at us, the shell landing close alongside, one to two feet to port and exploding. This ship had a three flag hoist up, which we could not make out, but took for recognition signal. We had hoisted the answering pennant and made reply. Send men on deck below to get ready to submerge, and stopped engines. I stayed on the bridge and began waving a flag. The next shell landed just forward of the bow and ricocheted over the bridge. Went below and submerged. The next shell hit the conning tower and about the same time one hit the steering stand. The next one hit the engine intake pipe. All started to leak. Secured lower conning tower hatch and flapper valves of others. Voice pipe from conning tower leaked badly. Valve would not close. Plugged voice pipe with potato masher and kept some of the water out. Headed away from firing ship until starboard motor controller shorted and blew circuit breaker, wireless started to spark and short circuit, when I blew tanks and sent men on deck with flags. Starting the engines we started from the firing ship. One destroyer gave chase. After getting tanks dry and reaching a position beyond the range of firing ship, I stopped engines and sending everyone on deck with lifepreservers and all available flags attempted to signal destroyer. She then swung broadside to and fired several broadsides, all falling short. Began signaling with whistle. The destroyer finally came within hail. And turned out to be the USS *Paul Jones* (DD-10).

The USS *H-3* ran aground near Eureka, California, in 1916. The cruiser USS *Milwaukee* tried to pull the submarine off and became stranded itself. The submarine was finally dragged across the sand spit to Humboldt Bay where it was relaunched. The cruiser was a total loss. This scene shows the efforts to drag the submarine over the sand to the bay. Seen here is the typical EB design feature of the bow cap on the torpedo tubes just above the man with the hat in the center. The bow planes are extended and just above on the deck the forward hatch is open. (US Navy SFLM)

In December 1917, the USS *F-1*, USS *F-3* and USS *F-2* found themselves making just such a test. In the five months since the United States entered World War I on the side of the Entente powers, the US Naval Submarine Force had been thrust into an unfamiliar role. Instead of combating enemy fleets trying to force the US coast, the boats were performing anti-submarine warfare patrols off the east coast of the US and off the Azores. There was little threat to the west coast so the remaining boats there were mostly holding training exercises.

The *F-2* was to seaward standing to the south on course 142°T about ten nautical miles off La Jolla light. The *F-3* was two points forward of the *F-2*'s port beam at a range of about 7,000yd. The *F-1* was about 2,000yd astern of the *F-3* on a bearing of 007°T from the *F-3*.

The F-Class had been designed without the bridge we see on later submarines. The crews had a pipe-and-rail rig onto which a canvas screen was lashed. This provided some protection from the wind and occasional spray. The captain and the officer of the deck (OOD) were on the bridge as well as two lookouts. About 1830hrs, the boats began to run into fog which soon became thick. The *F-1* changed course to 165°T to stand away from La Jolla and Point Loma. Being the aftmost boat, it would pass astern of the *F-3*. A radio message was sent to indicate the course change but it was evidently not received by either of the *F-1*'s companions. The OOD of the *F-2* was mindful of the two vessels on his port hand. At 1855hrs he turned the *F-2* to the west to clear the fog and to clear the area into which the *F-1* and the *F-3* would maneuver. The *F-2* would stand out to sea clear of the fog then turn north for the return trip along course 322°. Just after

1900hrs the *F-3* put on 10° right rudder and began a turn to a reciprocal course of 322°. The intention was to reverse course, run to the north out of the fog and back toward San Pedro. The assumption made was that the *F-1* was still to port and astern. The assumption was wrong.

The *F-3* struck the *F-1* on the port side near the bulkhead between the control and the engine room. The stiff stem of the *F-3* and the rounded torpedo-tube bow cap punched a 3ft wide by 10ft high hole in the upper hull of the *F-1*, driving all the way into the engine room. The *F-1* rolled to starboard, throwing all four men who were on the bridge into the sea. Unfortunately, the *F-3* pulled out of the hole because it had its screws running in reverse trying to stop. Not being pushed anymore, the *F-1* rolled back to port and started to flood fast. The man in the *F-1*'s conning tower, seeing the water coming in below him, climbed out and went over the side. No one else escaped. Someone in the engine room tried to open the hatch to get out but the ship was sinking fast and water pressure on the outside kept it shut until it was too late. Those in the forward end of the boat had no chance. Nineteen men went down with the ship. The five in the water were picked up by the *F-3* and it made its way back to San Pedro. The *F-1* became the Submarine Force's first wartime loss.

These weren't the only disasters to befall the Submarine Force during this period. Two submarines were victims of collisions with surface ships, the USS *S-51* in 1925 and the USS *S-4* in 1927. Their losses led directly to the invention and use of rescue chambers, escape trunks and rescue marker buoys. The USS *S-5* suffered an accidental flooding in 1920, but the crew was able to escape.

After World War I the L Class as well as prior classes had been made obsolete by the advances in submarine design and were quickly laid up and soon disposed of. Here the *L-9*, inboard, and *L-3*, outboard, await their demise. (US Navy)

The L-Class and operations during World War I

When the US entered World War I in 1917 its allies had been in the fight for nearly three years. They had, during those three years, been climbing the learning curve of submarine and anti-submarine warfare. Over the same three years, US submarine design had gone from the E-Class and F-Class, which originated in 1909 but current vessels of which were only one to two years old, through the O and R classes, which had been authorized and were being laid on the ways. However, this great advance in submarine operational capability could not be translated into first-line submarines for the US until late 1918 at the earliest and most likely not until 1920–21. Thus the US would have to go to war with what was available. That consisted of the A and B classes, now at Manila Bay; the three D-Class vessels which were not ocean-going boats; the F-Class and the E-Class which were small, but capable of crossing the Atlantic (the *F-4*, of course was not available, having been lost in 1915 off Honolulu); three H-Class boats which were operating off the west coast with the F-Class boats; the K-Class whose eight boats were split between east and west coasts; the L-Class boats which were just coming on line; and the N-Class which was also just being commissioned.

In October 1917, the USS *K-1*, USS *K-2*, USS *K-5*, USS *K-6*, and USS *E-1*, constituting SubDiv Four, assembled at Newport, Rhode Island, ready to cross the Atlantic. The crossing was horrible. They hit a storm on the second day out which scattered the group, and it was not until after the 27th that they all assembled in the Azores. The living conditions were

The USS L-1 alongside in Berehaven, Ireland, in 1918. L-Class boats were renumbered with an "A" (this boat was then AL-1) to differentiate them from Royal Navy L-Class submarines. The 3in/23cal Mk IX is seen on the forward deck. The engine room hatch is open aft. (US Navy)

not good as the tender had to leave to escort another group of boats. However, the sailors made the best of it and, on November 1, the *K-2* left for its first patrol.

On November 4, the second group of submarines to deploy left New York. It consisted of the little *E-1* and seven L-Class boats (the USS *L-1*, USS *L-2*, USS *L-3*, USS *L-4*, USS *L-9*, USS *L-10* and USS *L-11*) forming the Fifth Division. Their trip was even worse than that of the predecessors. The group was split up in a storm two days out. When the vessels arrived in the Azores they found the other boats barely able to keep things together, but making regular patrols in the area of the islands and out to 200 miles. This was a big area for the five small boats but they tried to keep up a good duty cycle. They had no support, no spares and no supplies and saw no enemy.

The Fifth Division, after spending a few days in the Azores, got under way for Queenstown, Ireland. As with its transit across the Atlantic, the division slammed head-on into a storm. It took eight days to get through. The *L-10* was separated from the remainder of the division and held forth against the storm, finally making Queenstown. It was during this transit that *L-10* lost a man overboard. GM1 R. A. Leese became the first US submarine casualty in a war zone. Lt E. W. F. Childs of the *L-2* became the second when he, as an observer, went down with HMS *H5* also operating out of Bantry Bay.

The *L-1*, now renumbered *AL-1* so its designation would not conflict with that used by the Royal Navy, made contact with a German submarine in May 1918 and fired two torpedoes. The US boat broached and was spotted by the German boat which was on the surface. The German boat twisted to avoid

the torpedoes and ran off, firing its deck gun at the struggling *AL-1*. A few days later, the *AL-11* fired two torpedoes at another U-boat a few miles away from the position of the *AL-1's* encounter. One torpedo broached then sank and the other detonated 200yd short of the U-boat.

By far the most peculiar engagement was the run-in the *AL-2* had with *UB-65*. On July 10, 1918, the *AL-2* was just south of Fastnet and spotted what was thought might be a surfaced submarine. After the object had been watched for a while, it disappeared. The OOD and lookout wondered if it was indeed a sub or just a floating piece of wreckage. Just at dusk, a torpedo exploded some 50yd from the US boat's stern. The lookout reported seeing a periscope just on the other side of the geyser. The explosion unseated the ventilation blowers and unclutched the engines. The captain, Lt P. F. Foster, ordered the rudder hard over and sounded the klaxon for dive. He hoped to come around full circle and ram the German sub. *AL-2* missed ramming but was close enough for the crew to hear the enemy screws through the hull. The C-Tube operator reported the position of the submarine contact and the captain brought the *AL-2* around to give chase. Then, the C-Tube operator

reported that there were two subs out there. The one ahead was slowing; then contact was lost. The other sub started to signal on its oscillator then signaled again. The *AL-2* turned toward the second boat and started to give chase underwater. The Germans, however, drew away with faster underwater speed and disappeared. The *AL-2* returned to the position of the loss of the first German submarine's contact and signaled on its oscillator using the same frequency and code the German boat had used. German records cite *UB-65* as a loss in the area in the time frame of this incident. It is assumed the German boat suffered its demise in one of two ways. Either it fired a torpedo which detonated prematurely and caused fatal damage, or the other German boat had fired at the *AL-2*, missed and hit the first boat. Either way, *UB-65* was lost in an engagement with the *AL-2*. Records show that the *AL-2* was credited by the British Admiralty with the destruction of the *UB-65* and the US Navy awarded Lt Foster a medal for the action. Thus, for the record the first US submarine to be officially credited with the sinking of an enemy submarine was the USS *AL-2* under the command of Lt Foster on July 10, 1918, just south of Fastnet Island. However, later analysis by the US Navy denied Foster and the *AL-2* official credit for the sinking.

After the armistice on November 11, 1918, the deployed submarines and their crews returned to the US, bringing with them new knowledge of submarine warfare. Submarine design and construction had advanced well beyond the little L-Class boats. The US was in the process of constructing the S-Class and had experimental fleet submarines both in the fleet and on the drawing board. There were engine problems to contend with and the U-boats that were turned over to the US Navy showed where some technical problems were and how they might be solved. In 1920 the Washington Treaty was signed, limiting the size of the world's navies. Most of the early classes were now taken out of commission and sold as being too old and no longer needed.

The early years of submarine design and operation were a steep learning curve which in many ways paralleled the early years of combat aircraft. Technology drove the design, problems with construction and operation drove the engineers to solve the issues that arose and that, in turn, often advanced technology. A submarine is a collection of technologies made to operate together in what has become one of the world's most complex mobile machines. We submariners like to think that our boats are, in fact, the most complex of all machines.

Some of the S-Class submarines formed part of the Lend-Lease arrangement early in World War II. This is the ex-USS *S-22*, which became HMS *P554*. It served as an ASW training boat for a couple of years before being sent back to the US. (US Navy)

INDEX

Note: numbers and letters in **bold** refer to plates and illustrations.